Before They Were President

BEFORE TEDDY ROOSEVELT WAS PRESIDENT

By Therese Shea

Gareth Stevens
PUBLISHING

Please visit our website, www.garethstevens.com. For a free color catalog of all our high-quality books, call toll free 1-800-542-2595 or fax 1-877-542-2596.

Library of Congress Cataloging-in-Publication Data

Names: Shea, Therese, author.
Title: Before Teddy Roosevelt was president / Therese M. Shea.
Description: New York : Gareth Stevens Publishing, 2018. | Series: Before they were president | Includes index.
Identifiers: LCCN 2017023785| ISBN 9781538210765 (pbk.) | ISBN 9781538210772 (6 pack) | ISBN 9781538210789 (library bound)
Subjects: LCSH: Roosevelt, Theodore, 1858-1919–Childhood and youth. |
  Presidents–United States–Biography.
Classification: LCC E757 .S54 2018 | DDC 973.91/1092 [B] –dc23
LC record available at https://lccn.loc.gov/2017023785

First Edition

Published in 2018 by
Gareth Stevens Publishing
111 East 14th Street, Suite 349
New York, NY 10003

Copyright © 2018 Gareth Stevens Publishing

Designer: Laura Bowen
Editor: Ryan Nagelhout/Kate Mikoley

Photo credits: Cover, pp. 1 (Teddy Roosevelt), 15 Stock Montage/Archive Photos/Getty Images; cover, p. 1 (battle scene) Library of Congress/Corbis Historical/Getty Images; cover, pp. 1–21 (frame) Samran wonglakorn/Shutterstock.com; p. 5 (main) Spartan7W/Wikimedia Commons; p. 5 (inset) Joe Ferrer/Shutterstock.com; p. 7 (father and mother) SimonATL/Wikimedia Commons; p. 7 (teddy bear) Marco Govel/Shutterstock.com; p. 9 Smith Collection/Gado/ Archive Photos/Getty Images; p. 11 PhotoQuest/Archive Photos/Getty Images; p. 13 Everett Historical/Shutterstock.com; p. 17 Aavindraa/Wikimedia Commons; p. 19 (parade) Bettmann/Getty Images; p. 19 (poster) Themadchopper/ Wikimedia Commons; p. 21 (Roosevelt) Tom/Wikimedia Commons.

Printed in China

CPSIA compliance information: Batch #CW18GS: For further information contact Gareth Stevens, New York, New York at 1-800-542-2595.

CONTENTS

Words in the glossary appear in **bold** type the first time they are used in the text.

AN AMERICAN WONDER

A man visiting the United States in the early 1900s said that the country had two natural wonders: Niagara Falls and President Theodore Roosevelt. As US president between 1901 and 1909, Roosevelt was different from past presidents. He was full of energy and very witty. People found him to be exciting.

Today, we picture a big man with small glasses, a **mustache**, and a loud laugh. But he wasn't always that way. He was once a sickly boy. His parents worried he wouldn't live to become an adult.

Presidential Preview

Throughout his life, Theodore Roosevelt showed he wasn't afraid to be unpopular with powerful people. He tried to make changes that would help ordinary Americans.

THEODORE ROOSEVELT BECAME THE US PRESIDENT, BUT HE ALSO HAD OTHER INTERESTS. HE WAS AN AUTHOR, SOLDIER, AND LATER, EXPLORER OF THE AMAZON RIVER!

NIAGARA FALLS

BABY TEEDIE

Theodore Roosevelt Jr. was born October 27, 1858, in his parents' home in New York City. His parents called him "Teedie." Though a noisy and active boy, he had **asthma** from a very young age. One of his earliest memories was waking up at night trying to breathe. His mother and father would rush to his side, doing everything they could to make him feel better.

Still, young Theodore was a lively boy. As a 3-year-old, according to his mother he was filled with mischief and had to be carefully watched.

Presidential Preview

Later, Theodore Roosevelt was sometimes called "Ted" or "Teddy." Toy stuffed bears were named "teddy bears" after him!

THEODORE ROOSEVELT SR.

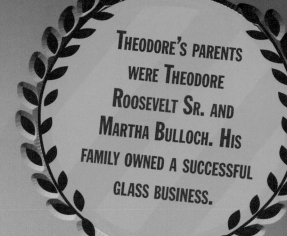

Theodore's parents were Theodore Roosevelt Sr. and Martha Bulloch. His family owned a successful glass business.

MARTHA BULLOCH

NATURE LOVER

The Roosevelt family spent summers in the country in New Jersey. Young Theodore grew to be a great lover of nature. He began a "museum of natural history" in his room. He even learned **taxidermy**!

Still, Roosevelt had days when he was so sick that he had to stay in bed. During those times, he read about animals or told his younger brother and sister adventure stories. He was ill so often that he didn't attend school. Instead, teachers came to his home.

Presidential Preview

As US president, Roosevelt set aside millions of acres of land so they wouldn't be spoiled. These areas became national forests.

In New York City, young Theodore once took off his hat to greet a woman. Several frogs leaped out from under it! He's shown here at about 10 years old.

9

BODY BUILDER

Young Theodore grew taller, but his health didn't improve. Even though he spent plenty of time outdoors, his parents noticed he was getting paler and thinner. His father gave him some advice: "You have the mind but you have not the body. . .You must make your body." He thought exercise would help his son overcome his illnesses.

From then on, Theodore Roosevelt Jr. did all he could to build up his strength. He lifted weights and did other exercises in the family's gym.

Presidential Preview

As US president, Theodore Roosevelt's visitors had a hard time keeping up with him. He took **ambassadors** on hikes!

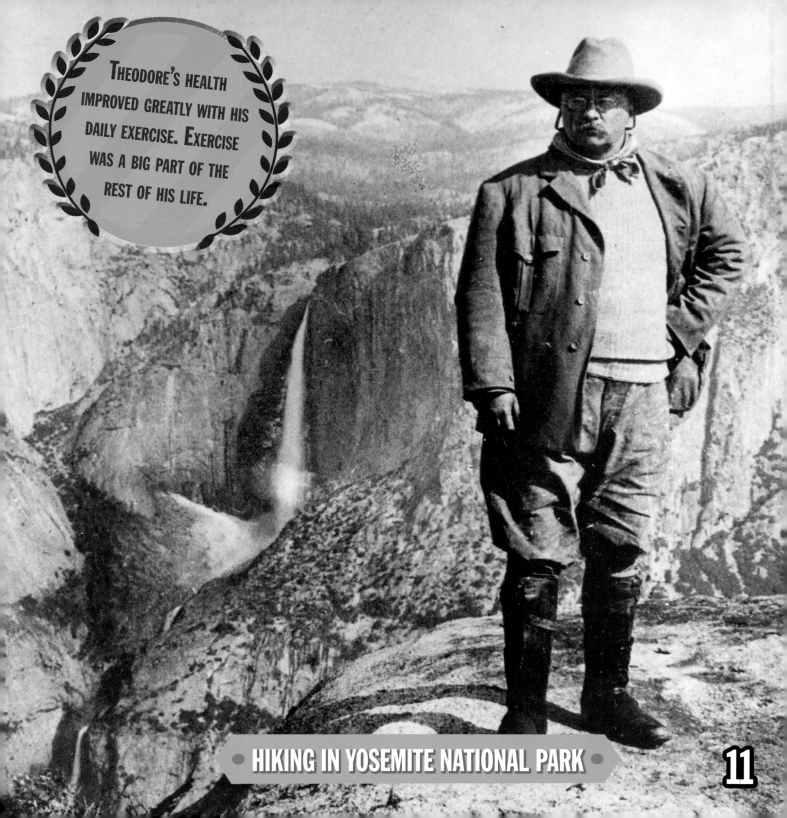

Theodore's health improved greatly with his daily exercise. Exercise was a big part of the rest of his life.

HIKING IN YOSEMITE NATIONAL PARK

A TOUGH TIME

When Roosevelt was older, he attended Harvard College. After he finished in 1880, he married Alice Lee and began Columbia Law School. Then, he decided to run for public office. He was elected to the New York State **Assembly** at the age of 23.

In 1884, Roosevelt's wife and his mother died on the same night. His sadness led him to leave the assembly and head to North Dakota to work on his **ranches**. He was even a **sheriff** there for a time.

Presidential Preview

During his time in the state assembly, Roosevelt fought **corruption** in the government. This made him popular with many people, but unpopular with those taking part in the corruption!

This photo was taken in 1885, after Roosevelt went to work on his ranch. He spent 2 years rounding up cattle and hunting there.

13

STARTING AGAIN

Theodore Roosevelt returned to New York in 1886. He married a childhood friend named Edith Carow. He also ran for mayor of New York City, but he lost the election.

Roosevelt held several positions in government over the next few years. He became police **commissioner** of New York City in 1895. He took on corruption in the police force. Sometimes, he walked the streets of the city at night in **disguise** looking for police officers acting illegally! Roosevelt also began the first US police academy.

Presidential Preview

Theodore Roosevelt wasn't the only one in his family to serve in the US government. Eleanor Roosevelt was his niece. She married a distant cousin, Franklin Roosevelt, who became president in 1933.

THEODORE AND EDITH HAD FIVE CHILDREN TOGETHER. ROOSEVELT ALSO HAD ONE DAUGHTER WITH HIS FIRST WIFE, ALICE.

ROUGH RIDER

In 1897, President William McKinley named Theodore Roosevelt assistant secretary of the US Navy. In 1898, the United States began a war with Spain after an American ship blew up off the coast of Spanish-controlled Cuba. Roosevelt helped prepare the US Navy to take on Spain's navy.

Then, Roosevelt left his post to take part in the war. He led a group of soldiers on horseback called the Rough Riders during the Battle of San Juan Hill in Cuba. Roosevelt was called a hero for his leadership.

Presidential Preview

In 2001, Theodore Roosevelt received a Medal of Honor for his role in the Spanish-American War.

The United States easily won the Spanish-American War. Here, Colonel Theodore Roosevelt is shown with his Rough Riders in Cuba.

17

GOVERNOR ROOSEVELT

Theodore Roosevelt became famous during the war. He was elected governor of New York in 1898. Again, he worked against corruption. Some people in power thought Roosevelt was too dangerous. They didn't want things to change. They needed to put Roosevelt in a position where they didn't think he could do them harm. So, they **nominated** him for vice president of the United States in 1900!

Roosevelt agreed to the nomination. He thought he had a greater chance to become president if he held that office.

Presidential Preview

Corrupt leaders had asked Roosevelt to run for governor because they knew he could win. However, they became upset that he "had the people's interest at heart" instead of theirs!

THE ADMINISTRATION'S PROMISES HAVE BEEN KEPT

1896

1900

Gone Democratic.

Gone Republican.

BANK

SAVINGS BANK

INTEREST PAID ON DEPOSITS

run on the Bank

A run to the Bank

THE
AMERICAN FLAG
HAS NOT BEEN PLANTED IN FOREIGN SOIL
TO ACQUIRE MORE TERRITORY
BUT FOR
HUMANITY'S SAKE"

Spanish Rule in Cuba.

American Rule in Cuba.

CAMPAIGN POSTER

ROOSEVELT LEADS A PARADE AS THE GOVERNOR OF NEW YORK.

THE 26TH PRESIDENT

Theodore Roosevelt became even more famous during the presidential election of 1900. He campaigned to be vice president for William McKinley, who was running for a second term as president. He traveled more than 21,000 miles (33,796 km) by train, and more than 3 million people saw him in person. He spoke in 567 cities in 24 states. McKinley and Roosevelt won easily.

On September 6, 1901, President McKinley was shot in Buffalo, New York, and died days later. Theodore Roosevelt was sworn in as the 26th president of the United States.

Presidential Preview

Theodore Roosevelt served nearly two terms, from 1901 to 1909. He ran again in 1912, but lost.

A Timeline of Teddy Roosevelt

1858 Theodore Roosevelt Jr. is born October 27 in New York City.

1880 Roosevelt graduates from Harvard College and marries Alice Lee.

1882 Roosevelt begins two terms in the New York State Assembly.

1884 Roosevelt's wife and mother die in February, and he leaves for the West.

1886 Roosevelt returns to New York and marries Edith Carow.

1895 Roosevelt becomes police commissioner of New York City.

1897 Roosevelt is named assistant secretary of the US Navy.

1898 Roosevelt leads the Rough Riders in the Spanish-American War and is elected governor of New York.

1900 Roosevelt is nominated for vice president of the United States.

1901 After William McKinley dies, Roosevelt becomes US president.

PRESIDENT ROOSEVELT

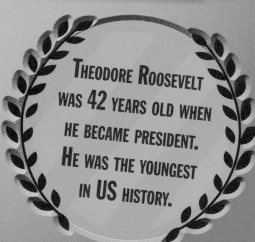

THEODORE ROOSEVELT WAS 42 YEARS OLD WHEN HE BECAME PRESIDENT. HE WAS THE YOUNGEST IN US HISTORY.

GLOSSARY

ambassador: a person sent to stand for their government's interests in another country

assembly: a group of people who make and change laws for a government

asthma: a condition of the body that makes it hard for someone to breathe

commissioner: an official who is in charge of a government department

corruption: dishonest or illegal behavior especially by powerful people

disguise: made to look like someone else

mustache: hair on a man's upper lip

nominate: to choose someone for a job, position, or office

ranch: a large farm where animals are raised

sheriff: an official who is in charge of making sure the law is followed in a place

taxidermy: preparing, stuffing, and mounting the skins of dead animals so that they look like they did when they were alive

Books

Burgan, Michael. *Who Was Theodore Roosevelt?* New York, NY: Grosset & Dunlap, 2014.

Uhl, Xina M. *Theodore Roosevelt.* Mankato, MN: The Child's World, 2016.

Wade, Mary Dodson. *Amazing President Theodore Roosevelt.* Berkeley Heights, NJ: Enslow Elementary, 2010.

Websites

Biography: President Theodore Roosevelt (Teddy)
www.ducksters.com/biography/uspresidents/theodoreroosevelt.php
Read more fun facts about this American president.

Theodore Roosevelt
www.whitehouse.gov/1600/presidents/theodoreroosevelt
Read a short biography of Teddy on the official White House website.

INDEX